Romancing the Blarney Stone
Rick Lupert

Ireland

Copyright © 2016 by Rick Lupert
All rights reserved

Rothco Press

Cover Design and Layout ~ Rob Cohen and Rick Lupert
Manuscript Design and Layout ~ Rick Lupert
Author Photo ~ Addie Lupert

"Somewhere Over Canada" and "Show Yourself Dublin" originally appeared in "Sappho's Torque".

This book is protected under the copyright laws of the United States of America. Any reproduction or other unauthorized use of the material or artwork herein is prohibited without the express written permission of the author except in the case of brief quotations embodied in critical articles and reviews.

First Edition ~ December, 2016

ISBN-13: 978-1-945436-04-8

Published by Rothco Press.
www.rothcopress.com

Visit the author online at
www.PoetrySuperHighway.com

When I die Dublin will be written in my heart.

- James Joyce

You're on Earth. There's no cure for that.

- Samuel Beckett

My passport's green.

- Seamus Heaney

Thank you Addie, Brendan, Elizabeth, Finbarr, People who would name their children *Finbarr,* Amber, Murray, Rodney, U2, Patrick Gehlan, Bus Driver Jerry, The Catholics, The Protestants, King John, The Giants, The Leprechauns, the good people at American Airlines, and Bernie, Sara, Greg and Mary for holding on to and transporting our child between states so we could leave the continent for a while.

To Addie who sees the Leprechaun in everyone.

Flying in my taxi

I want to Decorate the Plane

My window seat on the plane doesn't have a window.
They should tell you this when you book the flight.
A disclaimer would be nice. Something like
The window seats in this aisle don't have windows.
If I knew I was going to be seated by a wall
I would have brought a poster.

Cup of Catfee

The airplane magazine tells me all the cities which have both coffee and cats. None of these are cities which I live in, or am traveling to.
I will not rest until every establishment in Los Angeles has a kitten I can interact with.

Somewhere Over Canada

It is 7:30 in the morning and my eyes are
staging a revolution of closing hours.

I message Brendan to ask if he is awake
with a quick follow up telling him *I am not*.

They will not hold planes for tired people.
So if you wish to go to a place that is

different from the place you are in
you will need to defer to the schedules

of others. Behind me they discuss
the size of water bottles. This is a topic

I have nothing to add to. They say this
flight is nonstop but I can't imagine

any other kind.

Superfood

Oh surprise chunk of cheese
nestled beneath a forgotten bed of quinoa
and two overripe red pepper strands. You
have made all the difference today.

haiku

I'm pretty sure there's
quinoa on my chin all the
way to Chicago.

I Almost Forgot

The best thing about
having a window seat
is looking out and oh crap
it's still just a wall.

I Am Not Responsible for Air Travel

I hear the plane switching gears
like a bicycle or automobile switches gears
and not like a shift in a conversation
to a different topic on an agenda
and then it occurs to me that airplanes
may not have gears and this is much
more alarming than I was prepared for.

Language Non-Problem

I don't even know
how to mispronounce *croissant*
any more.

Nothing to Do

The best part about sitting at the wall seat on the plane is not having to stare out at the perceived infinity of the Earth's atmosphere.

P.S. Puffy clouds can suck it.

Planeservation

They have a hipster flight attendant
in first class. We have the full waist model.
I'm not even sure what that means.

Why IS This Wet?

I'm jarred from airplane sleep
by the phrase "why is this wet?"
A phrase all too commonly uttered
in the Lupert household and wherever
our six year old does roam.

Hello You

I'm trying to get some sleep but I keep thinking of things to write. Maybe if you stopped encouraging me by reading this I could finally get some shut-eye.

Romancing the Blarney Stone

Somewhere in this universe
in this solar system
on this planet
on another continent
in a country surrounded by water
in a town there
in a castle there
there is a stone
a known stone
a kissed stone
a stone kissed by
more men and women
than Caligula
My lips destined
for this stone
in that place
in all the places
that I mentioned
My lips
That stone
You'll see

Beastie Boy

I ask my son if he can play quietly.
He says *yes* but I know the real answer.
There'll be be no sleep 'til Brooklyn
which is unfortunate because that's
not where we're going.

A Delay in Chicago

The plane is here but
they can't find the crew.
I've spent so much
unintentional time
in Chicago.

I'm going to
get an iced tea.
I may blow my nose.
I can't imagine where
the crew is.

Taxi

We are taxiing to the runway.
I'm trying to find a poetic way

to tell you about the correlation
between this and the article in

the airplane magazine about
Harry Chapin who wrote a song

called *Taxi*.
It has lines such as

*Me, I'm flying in my taxi,
taking tips and getting stoned.*

I think he said it better.
You should take a break from

reading this to listen to that song.
I'll still be here when you get back.

Take all the time you need.

Stones

Thirty-five thousand feet above the east-west
and all of the Diet Cokes have been distributed.
A small group of people who know how to fly the plane
are flying the plane. The flight attendant is getting
frisky and passing out free Pringles to her favorite
passengers. She thinks no one will notice but I know
what is happening. I haven't wanted a *Pringle* in
thirty years. The announcements from the cockpit
are too quiet to fully hear. I make out the word
Syracuse and I'm not concerned about the context.
That is where I am going. That is where I will spend
the night. That is where I will scatter my mother in
the wind and rain before heading across the ocean
to kiss a stone I've never met.

Going

You all must be so proud of me.
So many pages in and I haven't
mentioned going to the bathroom once.

Time Zone Math

I
Addie is doing *time zone math* to determine
if having an apple with almond butter will ruin

dinner for her. She decides to do it. She uses
the words *right now* to demonstrate the urgency.

A naked toddler runs up the aisle chased by her mother.
Dinner is saved.

II
The flight attendant explains to the naked toddler
Gotta get your clothes on. No shoes, no shirt, no service.

As soon as Addie takes the first bite of her apple
I think to tell her *oh no we were going to have dinner*

at the end of the jetway in 20 minutes.
I don't say the words out loud though

because it is nicer not to,
and because

I am the only one at this altitude who
would think it's funny.

Syracuse

Something for Everyone in the Syracuse Airport

We are greeted by a sign that says "Telephones" and "Men" with an arrow pointing to the right.

Lesson Learned

Apparently even without a SIM card
cell phones can call *911*
I learn at two in the morning

after trying an internet-found trick
to make our Europe phone work
so the three Chittenango police officers

tell me.
They also want to know how much longer
I'll be in town.

Syracuse in June

is informed by
the end
of Hurricane Bill.
Bill is
such a strange name
for a hurricane.

Christmas Gift

Mary tells us the story of the package
she received last December.
So many other holiday gifts had arrived,
she accepted it with the grateful joy of
the season, not noticing at first, the official
United States Post Office sticker
labeled "Cremated Remains".
Welcome home mom.

Cemetery

I
Gophers are taking over the cemetery
were my grandparents are buried.
We have to avoid falling in their holes.
(the gopher holes)

II
Gregory cleans the headstones
(of our grandparents) with a brush he
had in the car for this kind of occasion.
He is prepared for any kind of occasion.

III
We open the box and return my mother
to her parents. It looks like her father
gets a little more. (Daddy's little girl)
The rain will finish the job of bringing
them back together.

IV
We say words.
Jewish words and other words.
(Not everyone wants to say words.)
We put stones on the headstones.

V
The white sand of my mother.
Now a blanket to her mother.
(and father.) Returned
to where she began.

Not Our Destiny

The shopping center outside downtown Syracuse is called *The Destiny Mall*. With that in mind we went there with certain expectations. These expectations are not met.

Meownifest Destiny

At my cousin's house in Chittenango
a cat comes to sleep with me.
How is it that cats know exactly
what to do and who to do it with?

We discuss how things don't come with enough holes.

They are referring to planters and water drainage, but, you know, whenever someone mentions a hole plants are not the first thing on my mind.

Aww Man-lius

I ask Tara
who lives in Manlius
if every time something
goes wrong, she says
Aww Man...lius.
She says she has
never done that but
she's willing to
give it a try.

Junior High School Reunion

Everyone in DeWitt Wegman's is someone
I could've gone to junior high school with.
I want to have a reunion so bad but I
haven't seen them since 1982 and I
have no way of knowing who they are.

I want to put a sign around my neck that says
"Hello I am Rick Lupert from Syracuse. I live
in California now. Please identify yourselves
I want to reminisce about the past. I want to
give you a hug."

It feels like a lot to put on a sign,
and by the time I figure this out
I'm already waiting in the
Syracuse airport for a plane
to Dublin.

Actually it's a plane to Philadelphia,
but I'd rather not get into the details.
Oh friends from another life,
wherever you are, whatever you look like,
we'll have to plan ahead next time.

They Live Near Here

I tell Addie on our stopover in Philadelphia
we should message her parents and tell them
We're at the airport, and ask if they going to pick us up?
Certainly someone would find this funny.

All the Time

The TSA are not in a hurry
at the Syracuse *International* Airport
(I hear they go to Canada).

Muscle Memory

We haven't taken a plane from the east coast to begin out vacation in several years. I wonder if we'll remember how to do it?

Reverse Order

We take a photo of us under the *Welcome to Syracuse* sign as we prepare to leave Syracuse. We couldn't get it together to do that when we arrived. We'll Photoshop Jude in later.

This Book Gets Interactive!

While waiting to board, the airport TV shows a CNN story about how a terror attack is a serious possibility. This is kind of like playing *Jaws* for everyone at the beach, or *Airport* movies for in-flight entertainment, or *Super Size Me* to people eating at McDonalds. Feel free to use the space below to add your own examples.

_____

_____

_____

_____

_____

_____

_____

_____

We have front row seats on the plane to Philadelphia.

We are kings of the world.
(Addie is the queen.)

Nostalgia

I can't come to Syracuse without
imagining living here again.
As the plane lifts away
As I see all the places I've known
I think *what a small town,*
what a manageable town.
Goodbye mom.
I will be back.

I Can See What's Coming

When we fly over Allentown, Pennsylvania
I see everything about that town I know.
The airport, the farmer's market
Dorney Park, Wegman's. Addie's parents' house
The hospital where she was born.

You'll hear more about Allentown
in nine days.

35,000 Feet

I see a car going somewhere.
Where's it going? Probably
not Dublin.

In the Philadelphia Airport

Every time I see a *Legal Seafoods*
I want to break every law I can
that involves fish.

No Class

I try the old trick of asking the airline person working the gate if they have the *cute young looking couple upgrade to first or business class.* She says *no.* Actually that old trick has never worked. I'm not even sure it's a real trick.

First Contact

I
An Irish family on our flight
has a daughter named Brooklyn.
If we have a daughter I'm going
to name her Dublin.

II
I want to tell them we're going to Dublin
and ask if they will tell us any Irish secrets
they think we should know. I'd promise to
keep it hush hush.

Author's Credit Due

Addie wonders if one particular flight attendant is Irish.
She thinks so because he *looks like a giant leprechaun.*

When she notices me writing this down she threatens
to not say anything for the rest of the trip.

This is quickly negated when she goes on to tell me
all he needs is to be dressed in green, and wearing

a little green hat, and to be *this big.*
(She demonstrates the size with her hands.)

I have a feeling we'll be hearing a lot more
from Addie on this trip.

Blanketfest Destiny

Addie is now doing a survey of the airplane blanket colors at the other seats. She noticed a purple one nearby and she has dark grey. She wants a purple one.

Dublin Day 1

Aer Lingus

Don't get me started on
the implications of the name
of the national airline here.

haiku

Landing in Dublin
Out the window, Ireland
owns the color green

Bus Into Town

Sign in the Dublin tunnel says
Keep two chevrons apart.
Does anyone know how long
a chevron is? Is it similar to a Texaco?

Not Iceland

The boy in Dublin wearing the shirt that said
Iceland is one of the first things we see.
We're not falling for that again.

Sushi in Dublin

The sushi restaurant
offering *American-style Sushi*
may be missing the point.

Hoping for Green Mummies

We're off to the National Leprechaun Museum where I'm sure to see the taxidermied and/or mummified remains of historic and/or ancient leprechauns.

Napkinfest Destiny

I'm pretty sure Addie has hummus on her nose.
Either that or it's Irish leprechaun fairy dust.
Either way she wants it wiped off.

In the Leprechaun Museum

I
Because of my participatory nature
the tour guide has declared me her favorite.

II
She instructs us not to leave the *Giants Room*
until she comes to get us.

III
We are left in the *Giants Room* for a long time.
It's how the Irish diminish the cockiness if its tourists.

IV
They say most leprechauns live with their mothers
for hundreds of years, which is why you never see
female ones. But where did the mothers come from
I ask you?

V
Leprechauns are a third the size of humans.
Humans are a third the size of giants.
I personally fit somewhere between
leprechauns and humans.

VI
We pass through a *rainbow*
which feels like a bunch of colored strings
hanging from the ceiling, but it does end
with a pot of gold.

VII
They say the leprechauns are
the accountants of the faeries.
I wonder who their lawyers are?

VIII
There's a whole lot about faeries
on the leprechaun tour and you don't
even have to pay extra for it.

IX
People unexpectedly throw money in the pot of gold room
even though they specifically have a wishing-well room later on.
Human beings will throw money into any hole they encounter.

X
The man in the store at the Leprechaun Museum
apologizes for the sunny weather. Says *Irishmen are
wandering about in shorts.* Says *no-one should
have to see an Irishman's knees.*

She May Hop Anyway

For a brief moment Addie thinks the *Ha'Penny Bridge* is actually called the *Hopping Bridge*. There is a measurable decrease in her excitement when I tell her the real name.

Attention Needed

We pass by a sign that says
Press Button For Attention
I've been going about it
the wrong way this whole time.

Waiting for the Irish Whiskey Museum Tour to Start

We haven't slept in at least twenty-four hours.
This can't possibly be a good idea.

Notes from the Irish Whiskey Museum

I
Uisce Beatha
is Gaelic for water of life.
The first word became
whiskey.

II
According to *apocrathytical* monks
who lived hundreds of years ago:
*What whiskey can't cure
can't be cured.*

III
Twelve people died during the
Dublin whisky volcano which

led to a fire which was abated
by rings of horse manure.

Guess what they died from?
Drinking dirty street whiskey.

IV
I hiccup during the whiskey tasting
which causes the docent to give me special attention.
He's already singled me out with a warning
to not drink dirty whiskey from the street.
I wish I were making that up.

Day Life in Dublin

Temple Bar Square
doesn't seem as clean as
the piazzas in Rome.
But it's just as alive.

Pole Position

There's a pole in the middle of Dublin
I'd like to think of it as a pole but *Wikipedia* says
it's a spire. I don't know what the pole is for.

I've asked Addie multiple times and she doesn't know.
We've been taking a lot of pictures of the pole.
The pole from a distance.

The pole up close.
Us with the pole on the background.
(There're a lot of those.) We're getting to the point where

after another picture with the pole, she'll say
Are we done with the pole yet? How can one ever
be done with the pole?

It's the largest pole I've ever seen.
(It's, really, an impressive pole.)
There's no information near the pole

about what the pole is, or who it's for,
or who put it up. It's just a large pole on O'Connell Street.
It's too thin to be a building, but it's taller than most buildings.

WHAT IS THIS POLE FOR?
I could read the rest of the *Wikipedia* article
but I didn't come all the way to Dublin

just to search the internet
for Irish Poles.
POLE!

Hickey's Pharmacy on O'Connell Street Only Treats One Thing.

(It's hickeys.)

Show Yourself Dublin

Two days without sleep.
Our feet have quit their jobs.
Potatoes of every kind inside us.
At least three kinds of whiskey.
Dublin is a city like other cities.
They pick up the trash.

They erect their spires.
They move you from one room
to the other if you don't like the smell.
There are three more days to
come out of your shell, Dublin.
Wake us up. Shine for us.

People have been telling us
not to kiss the stone, but
we've come all this way, I feel
we're going to kiss the stone.
We can no longer see the river
from our hotel window.

Dublin Day 2

Old Shirt

Addie suggests that
I buy a new shirt
after she sees me put on
the nice short sleeved
button down I've been wearing
since before we met in 2002.
"You don't like it" I ask her.
All she'll commit to is
It's fine.

Containment

I
Next trip I need to bring more bags
Addie says. Her love of things to contain
other things will not be contained.

Boxes, Tupperware, Pyrex, water bottles.
Don't get me started on her convulsions when
we pass by *The Container Store*.

II
We just finished putting breakfast inside us.
We, irreplaceable human containers.
Day two In Dublin begins.

Freebird Records

bills itself as a secret book and record store.
People have to stop putting "secret" on their signs
if they want to be taken seriously.

In the Little Museum

I
1916
Fighting would stop one hour each day
so James Carney, the park keeper
could feed the ducks.

II
The spire is called
The Monument of Light,
a competition winner
known locally as
Stiletto in the ghetto
Spire in the mire
Stiffy by the Liffey

III
Never let the truth
get in the way of
a good story.

IV
I score 235 on the *Grip Test* in the Little Museum
Grip Test Machine. I'm not sure what that means
but I'm satisfied with the result.

V
They tell us The Pole
which is really The Spire
which is really the Monument of Light
was erected (haha) after the I.R.A.
blew up the (thing that was there before).
Ireland's army tried to finish the job
but only ended up blowing out all the the windows
on O'Connell street, leaving the base intact and
otherwise un-blown up. I wish the first thing
was still there because you could go up it.
You can only look at the spire which I prefer
to call the pole. I do so love to go up things.
I'm more indifferent about poles.

VI
I hear echoes of my formative years
in the U2 exhibit. Bono said *when you
see a mansion in America, you think,
someday that could be me. When you
see a mansion in Dublin, you say
I'm gonna get that bastard.* U2
successfully hired as the greatest band
in the world.

VII
A sign says *Make Sure of Alfie First*.
I'm going to find out who Alfie is
and then live by these words.

VIII
The Little Museum in Dublin
is a little bigger than little.
(but not a lot)

IX
The sign that, I think, says
"The introduction of Internet in Ireland"
Actually says "The introduction of internment
In Ireland". I really need to have my eyes checked.
And my brain.

X
Christy Brown
Irish writer
with only the use of his left leg
wrote books with just that foot
Immortalized in film
His words his legacy
Choked to death on food in England
Neglect suspected (wife Mary)
Needed the oxygen of family and Dublin
Was uncontainable

XI
Oh the sound of the toilet
in the little museum in Dublin.
Like a minimalist waterfall.
Like something Japanese.

P.S. I'm talking about the one in the second floor,
NOT the top floor, in case you want to see it for yourself.

P.P.S. The one on the left.

XII
The woman waiting to get into the toilet
after me asks if it's unisex. I tell her it's
every sex you can imagine. I'm not sure
if her laughter is awkward or if it's just
her imagination at work.

Every Little Irish Baby

Their hair like an explosion of carrots
wheeled about on St. Stephens Green.
Their hands pushing up little sunglasses.
Their eyes with the fire of leprechauns.

Walk!

The sudden chirping sound
of the walk sign when it's time to walk
startles us back to 2015.

They Never Have Me in Mind

One store has a sign advertising
"We buy everything." Didn't take long before
I came up with a list of things they
were not willing to buy.

Baby, You Can't Drive My Car

Addie sees a child driving a car
until she remembers cars are different here
and realizes that's not what she saw at all.

At the Guinness Storehouse

Céad míle fáilte
100,000 welcomes

I
I dip my hand into a vat of Barley
not knowing if I'm allowed to.

II
Arthur Guinness signed a nine-thousand year lease
for the property upon which he built his brewery.

III
I touch the water
not knowing if I'm allowed to.

IV
They say Arthur is the magical fifth ingredient
of Guinness. The one ingredient I can't touch.

V
We're told to remember *there's a little bit of Arthur in every pint.*
I guess I'm going to have to suspend my vegetarianism
for the free pint at the end of the tour.

VI
An arrow lies and we walk into a corner.

VII
They say the strain of yeast used today is descended
from the original strain that Arthur Guinness used.
It may not be true. But they do say it. A yeast family tree
must be out of control.

VIII
The brewers today asks the question
Would Arthur be happy?

IX
Part of a barrel is called the *butt*.
I have no doubt that would be my son's favorite part.

X
Addie spends a lot of time in the barrel making exhibit.
It must be a container related thing.

XI
The story of transporting Guinness
is the story of transportation itself.
Which is why I always have one
while driving to work.

XII
The Guinness storehouse developed its own in-house railroad in 1853.
I'd tell you more but I just came across a sculpture that's breathing and
I have to pay attention to that now.

XIII
There is a list of instructions
on the escalator to the second floor
none of which are *get on escalator*
and ride to the top.

XIV
Addie asks, as we approach the tasting room,
if I want to have a tasting. In this place at this time,
it's like asking a sculpture if it wants to
continue to breathe.

XV
I see people with yarmulkas
in line ahead of us at the tasting experience.
I'm now sure that either Guinness is kosher,
or these men have strayed from the flock.

XVI
They say the Guinness tasting room
*is a magical experience where all
your senses will come to life.*
I have no idea what I've been sensing
for the last forty-six years.

XVII
Nothing says Guinness like a Guinness hair brush
is the main lesson I learn in the Guinness advertising exhibit.

XVIII
The one dark tunnel leading into the tasting room...
aww never mind it's time to taste beer.

XIX
A fish riding a bicycle tells me
a woman needs a man like a fish needs a bicycle
which tells me everything.

XX
They have a Guinness Academy here, but we aren't admitted
because our grades aren't good enough.

XXI
The urinals here are too tall for children.
I realize that not that many children come here.
They are all out driving the cars that Addie is seeing.

XXII
The sample message on the pint glass says *your message here*
which is exactly what I want my message to say.

XXIII
We take seats in the *Gravity Bar* overlooking the city.
I take the one with the view of the city and Addie
takes the one with the view of a baby.

There are photographic opportunities everywhere.
My beer is the *Foreign Extra*. Addie has the *Draught*.
A third of the way in and mine is doing its job.

We see the mountains where the water comes from.
The beer water, not the general purpose water.

Seats on the seventh floor are a hot commodity.
We've scored a couple and we feel rich.
One or two more sips and I won't need a seat to feel rich.

I could sit here for nine-thousand years.
I could baptize babies in the Liffey.
I could bust a spring of Wicklow water.

I'm feeling this right now.

XXIV
The Guinness Storehouse teaches you about beer
unlike the *Heineken Experience* in Amsterdam which
felt like an amusement park that also had beer.

XXV
Everyone is happy in the Gravity Lounge
with their pints of Guinness. Everyone except
for the baby whose pacifier isn't cutting it.

XXVI
I salute the views of Dublin.
That may just be the beer saluting.

XXVII
They say Guinness is best served at six degrees celsius.
I say it is best served in a glass.

XXVIII
No one compliments me on my choice of wearing a Guinness t-shirt to the Guinness Storehouse. I guess they're used to this kind of thing.

XXIX
Addie is researching dinner.
She looks up from the phone and says
I don't care if they have a small vegetarian
section on their menu, we are NOT going
to a steak house. I have spoken.

I want to find her a microphone
so she can drop it.

XXX
Does the Guinness family still own the company
I ask no one in particular as I type this into the phone.

XXXI
We have waited for our turn to sit down.
Now we are sitting down. Soon we will get up
and it will be somebody else's turn.
This is the circle of life at the Guinness Storehouse.

XXXII
We can see the pole from up here.
I have a feeling I'll be seeing that pole
for a long time, wherever I go.

XXXIII
I try to find the best angle
to jump off the Gravity Lounge
in case such a need should arrive.

XXXIV
Apparently *hurling* is a sport here in Ireland.
I'm quite sure after all of this Irish whiskey
and beer, I'll be quite good at it.

XXXV
I see a girl with a Guinness head mustache
which may be the greatest thing I've ever seen.

XXXVI
At the store in the Guinness Storehouse
you can get anything with the word Guinness on it
including a teabag holder, which is weird and crazy,
and, honestly, I'm experiencing a lot of emotions thinking
about a Guinness teabag holder. Oh shit, there's coffee mugs too.
I'm going to need some time alone to work this all out.

I Want to Walk

I try pressing every stump and pole I can find
to activate the walk signal. Addie tries the actual button
which seems to have a better effect.

Liffeyism

I invent a phrase for when you are sure about something while walking along Dublin's river. *Absoliffey*.
There aren't enough mics to drop.

The Struggle Continues

Autocorrect wanted to change *mics* to *mice* in that last poem. I want you all to know I would never drop mice.

Oversimplification

In *Game of Thrones* terms, essentially, the Irish are the Wildlings.

On the Way to Dinner

I
I can only imagine the explosion of cultures
that happens at *Monty's of Kathmandu* restaurant.

II
I don't know what the *King Kong Club* is
but I want to know more than anything.

III
One store sells infant perambulators.
The same one sells breakfast dresses.

Or all of this is a hunger induced fantasy
on the way to dinner.

At Fallon & Byrne

I
The French waiter tells Addie there is meat in the soup.
But he means wheat. They meet in the middle with
the word *bread*.

II
I keep wanting to applaud
like a Pavlovian dog
every time they applaud at the retirement
party at the next table

III
Addie says I may not eat spoonfuls
of the orgasmic Fallon & Byrne branded
French butter.

She also does not think it would be
a good idea to add the butter as a
third party to our marriage.

IV
We have to adjust our table position
several times to deal with the situation
in which the serving staff seem unaware
that our bodies, that they keep connecting with
are attached to human beings who have
the ability to have physical sensations.

Bathroomfest Destiny

Yes you can use the restroom here.
even though you are not dining here right now
because we are Irish and we love you.

We Pass by the Superdry Store

Everything just seemed kind of regular dry.

Keep Change in Your Pocket

All those times crossing the Ha'penny Bridge
in just two days. I'm glad they don't charge anymore.
Those ha'pennies really add up.

Sleeping La Vida Loca

It is the end of the day
but revelers outside our hotel room
are living *La Vida Loca*.

We think it's a barbecue
the hotel is putting on but
our feet don't want to hear it.

I've spent a half hour
(that's an exaggeration)
with a hair dryer pointed in my shoe.

Tomorrow it's heavy art
and I'm not talking about lifting
and a book so old

no-one has touched it for years.
I'm going to adjust the temperature
in our room.

Or not.
We're told everyone learns Irish
but hardly anyone speaks it.

All the road signs
are in English and Gaelic though.
In case I wasn't clear

Irish is Gaelic.
Maybe the temperature is alright.
It is after midnight here

and other times
on other continents
where people we know

are in the throws of their day.
Our day has been thrown.
It is sailing through the air.

It is about to land.
It may have already landed.
This is all the thud.

Dublin Day 3

At the Bakehouse

I
We switch coffees twice at breakfast.
Addie wants me to have the more filled one.
But then she thinks the less filled one might
be stronger. She only wants the best for me.
I go with the potential for strength and
it turns out this Americano could lift a car.
Hers could too. I'm going to look into Americanos
back home in America where they
also call them *Americanos*.

II
There are forty-four rolling pins
on the wall at The Bakehouse on
Bachelors Walk, just a ha'step or two
east of the Ha'Penny Bridge.
I counted them so you wouldn't have to.

III
The niceness of the Irish people
has its central nexus at the Bakehouse
where the waitresses couldn't stop smiling
even if you rearranged the wall display of
rolling pins.

IV
When I order coffee in any country
I don't want them to ask me to clarify it.
I just want them to give me whatever they
think coffee is.

V
I startle the waitress when I approach
the counter asking for glasses of water.
I startle her again when I ask her to add
ten percent to the bill for tip. No one wants
to do math and I have have become the
Creature from the American Lagoon.
I tell her, after the first startle, that it
happens often with me, even when
they see me coming.

Notes at Trinity college

I
You can get married in the chapel at Trinity College
if you are both graduates of the college, and if it is
within five years of graduating, or, as our tour guide
tells us, *you have to really have your life together.*
She assures us she will definitely not be getting
married here.

II
The old Provost George Salmon (1888-1904)
fought all his life to not allow women to study here.

When he was forced to sign the papers to allow them in,
he said he signed with his hand, but not with his heart.

He died of a heart attack
a few months later.

Today graduating women fling their caps
at his stature in disgust. It's tradition.

III
The maple trees here are from Oregon.
They grow bigger here because of the rain
and because of the four hundred dead monks
they are planted on top of.
sanctified fertilizer.

IV
If you live on campus you can apply
to have a work of art from the College's collection
hang in your room. Our guide's friend had a Picasso
drawing in hers. I never should have dropped out.

V
Courtney Love and
Winston Churchill
both spoke here.
Not on the same day.

Peacocknizant

We're in line to see the *Book of Kells*.
I overhear the guide in line behind us
say something about peacocks. I missed
the context, but I am intrigued.

The First Stanza of a Poem About a Cat by an Irish Monk from St. Gallen, Switzerland That was on the Wall at the Book of Kells. (I'm pretty sure it's in the public domain now. [Please don't sue me ancient Irish monks!])

I and Pangur Bàn my cat
'Tie a like task we are at:
Hunting mice is his delight,
Hunt my words I sit all night.

No Noes

The young man
in the Douglas Hyde gallery
almost *nices* us to death
as he explains why
the college's art collection
is not on display
to the public.
The last thing
an Irishman wants to say
is "no" to a visitor.

I'm Determined to Have an Irish Coffee But There are Issues

It's an alcoholic drink so I can't take it to go.
Addie can't bring her salad from next door into the pub,

and, late at night, when we have all the time in the world
it is too late to have a coffee drink.

Addie tells me she doesn't want to send me into the pub
by myself to drink one because she may never see me again.

We head to the National Gallery,
salad in hand, Irish coffee in head.

At The National Gallery

I
Master of the Youth of at Romold
R Brabant, c.1490

We're not sure if the men are bald
or wearing hats.

What makes the most sense to us is neither.
They have shaved the centers of their heads.

II
The Immaculate Conception
Ginúint Mhuire gan Smál, 1660

Mary
cupping her own breasts
seems to be stepping on three children.
A guy with a large fishhook nearby.

III
The Virgin Mary had a little lamb.
Something to look into.

IV
Victorious Love
An Grá Saolta go Caithréimeach, c.1625

Evil Cupid
has a pointy dick
hovering over
musical instruments and
chopped off foot.

V
A Wooded Landscape - the path on the dyke
Meindert Hobbema, 1663

Cows back then
looked pretty much the same
as they do today.
(Maybe a little more muscular)

VI
Peasant Wedding
Pieter Brueghel the Younger, 1620

The first appearance of Hobbits
in a painting.

VII
A Family
Louis le Brocquy, 1951

What attracts me most in this painting
of three naked family members
is the cat, also nude
as cats are.

VIII
I want to assemble
all the missing body parts
from the paintings.

The top of the woman's head from
Van Dongen's *Stella in a Flowered Hat*,
the missing leg from Nathanial Hone's *The Conjurer*.

Maybe grab the foot from *Victorious Love*
and make my own person, a *penny dreadful*
to display during business hours.

The rest of the time will be his
to do with as he pleases.

IX
Most of the National Gallery is
not accessible because of renovation.

There's a *Masters of the Collection* exhibit
that has a single Monet, which is better than
no Monet at all.

There's a video showing the expansiveness
of the main galleries.

So many countries to see, that video
may be all we get.

X
The National Gallery offers
Creative Writing Kits you can
take with you while visiting.
I don't bother since I already
have one with me.
(I'm talking about my brain.)

Dental Technology

They have interdental brushes for cleaning between teeth which makes dental floss seem like something only cavemen would use.

Roinn an Taoisigh

The sign in Irish says
Roinn an Taoisigh.

Translated it says
Department of the Taoiseach

which, thankfully,
cleared it all up for me.

At the Port House

I
Addie tells me to put the camera and the fork away
for reasons that I can't fully explain but I know for
sure they involve a now-empty large glass of sangria.

II
The path to the bathroom
is lined with full wine bottles
an entire wall high.

III
Addie almost puts on a wax mustache
made from our table's candle drippings.
But decides against it when she sees me
reaching for the camera.

IV
When I see under the alcohol-free menu
a *nojito* I laugh like humor has just been invented.
Thank you sangria!

V
We have been personally attended to
by at least four different staff members.
It gets awkward when one asks if
we'd like anything else and we have
already ordered from another.
They should have more intra-dinner service meetings.

VI
A party of six sits down in the sacred cave.
But gets up to leave almost immediately.
Such a shame. We would have died to
have been seated in the cave.

On the Dublin Literary Pub Crawl

> *Ireland, an island behind an island,*
> *the afterthought of Europe.*
> ~James Joyce

I
I dare Addie to stand up
in the middle of the next scene
and ask the actors
"are you guys serious?"
She refuses.

II
The Old Stand is "possibly the oldest pub in Ireland"
according to a message on their cash register.
It's also possible that it is not, according to
a common sense interpretation of
that cash register's assertion.

III
The literary pub crawl was scheduled
to go on for two and a quarter hours.
At three hours it was still going strong
and in fact it may still be happening.

IV
The tour ends at *The Davy Byrne*
where an entire chapter of Ulysses
was set in exchange for eliminating
Joyce's bar tab there.

It's Alright Irishmen

An Irishman
is most likely
to begin
a conversation
or encounter
with the word
"sorry."

Again, I Can't Read

I misread a sign that says "Youth illuminator" as "Youth Eliminator" which almost sounds like an Arnold Schwarzenegger film and definitely sounds like a bad idea.

I Keep Getting Irish Stuff on Me

First the puddle of something spilled
maybe a shake or who knows,
bled through my right shoe.
Had to wash it out at the hotel.
Spent a half hour with the hair dryer.

Then melted wax
poured off the table at the tapas place
also landed on the right shoe.
Didn't notice 'til later, and when I saw it
panicked, thinking it was something
less wholesome than dried wax.

Then *something* on my forearm.
Probably from leaning against a wall on the tour.
I'd describe it to you, but
you'd probably stop reading.

Home Remedy

Addie instructs me to swish whiskey
around the inside of my mouth to help
fend off a potential cold-sore.
Neither of us have any idea if it will work
but I'm sure willing to give it a try.

Finbarr

We hang out with Finbarr, the guide, after the tour.
He is twenty-eight years old, or, *in that ball park*
and has a beard like an *evil Moses*.
He's a cat guy which diffuses that a bit.
He is *classic Finbarr* and we are not at all
jealous that he gets free pints at every pub.
He laughs like an Irishman.
Refers to me kindly as *Richard Dreyfus*.
Leaves to bring a pizza to his girlfriend.
What does he do when he's not leading a tour?
Sleep he says. Which is exactly what we
go back to our hotel and do.
Sleep.

Dublin Day 4

Memories of Portland (Maine)

The seagulls are making their presence known through our hotel windows. It's not like the ever-present Portland, Maine ones you may have read about on pages 164, 169, 175, 186, 196, 206, 209, 214, 241, 261, and 285 of my previous book *Professor Clown on Parade* but they're making a solid effort.

At Queen of Tarts

We dine at a table surrounded by butternut squash
and apples that are making a valiant effort to
look like pears. Halfway through the meal
a man emerges from the kitchen and with
a Dublin *sorry* reaches his hand around us
and takes two of the squash away. Lunch
is coming. This is how you want it to be.
The fruits and vegetables not decorative
but functional. Like you've wandered into
a gingerbread house, and you spend your life
eating and rebuilding
eating and rebuilding.

Sorry

We stand in front of Trinity College
So we can take a picture of me
Ma*rick*ulating.

Notes From the Historical Dublin Walking Tour

Dublin is like a prostitute...
~Oscar Wilde

I
The guide tells us once we get the green man
we will all *skip across the road diagonally.*
Most of us just walk but the image is delightful.

II
The *Long Room* in the Old Library in Trinity College
is the inspiration for the Jedi Library in Star Wars
Insert clever comment about the *force* here.

III
The white polka dots
on the red ribbons
around the maple trees
in front of The Wax Museum
must mean something.

IV
Dublin is the city of vanishing statues.

V
The scholar leading the tour
tells us about one of Dublin's great bathrooms
built in the vaults of an old bank building.
So it's not just me.

VI
No one knows the relevance of General Wolftone's
large nose.

VII
We pass by *Oscar* and *Golden Globe* statues
in Temple Bar. As a representative of Hollywood
I take over the tour in case anyone has any questions.

VIII
We are promised the *Naked German of Dublin*.
The brochure didn't advertise nudity but it
doesn't go un-appreciated.

IX
Everyone takes a picture of the *Naked German of Dublin*.
Especially me. The guide tells us when it was erected and
I giggle with my secret knowledge of what he just said.

X
One of the newest buildings
is also one of the most reviled
built on the un-excavated remains
of Vikings.

XI
Christ Church Cathedral
has many things including
the fossilized remains
of a cat and a mouse
discovered in an organ.

XII
Dubh Linn
Viking for
dark waters.

XIII - haiku
We're told Bram Stoker
had one of the finest beards
in Irish history.

XIV
Our guide talks a lot about beards.
But he acknowledges this and
we're all okay with it

XV
The streets are named for what they did there
Cows Lane featured butchers.
Market Street had markets.
I'll let you imagine what happened
on Love Lane.

XVI
You don't have a rebellion when it's raining.

XVII
The Irish proclamation of independence
mentioned her *exiled children in America*
referring to millions of Irish Americans.

XVIII
A terrible beauty is born
Oscar Wilde after 1916
when the twentieth century
Troubles began.

Hopping In Dublin

I
They refer to their happy hour
as *hoppy hour* which may
be the must genius thing
I've ever seen.

It's also possible someone
just turned the chalk "a" into an "o".

II
We tell Will on the Literary Pub Crawl
he should use Hop-Stop to find his way
back to wherever he is going. He
thinks we're referring to the local
Hop on Hop Off bus tours. This
is never clarified and we think Will
may have hopped into the Liffey.

III
At one point
for some reason
Addie hopped.
I have a picture
of it.

LiteraryFest Destiny

We head to the Dublin Writers Museum
where I will take my rightful place.
(Which will be outside the facility
once they realize who I am.
[Or who I am not...])

Notes at the Dublin Writers Museum

I
The Dublin Writers Museum is next door to
the most expensive restaurant in Dublin
which is ironic since no writer
could afford to eat there.

II
Jonathan Swift's *Gulliver's Travels*,
a biting satire of the society of its day,
features a land of giants who
still frighten me in my day.
#EmbraceMyLilliputionism

III
Stoker's *Dracula* in 1897
was based on *Carmilla*
by Joseph Sheridan Le Fanu.
I'm going to have to look into that.

IV
Remind me to read
George Bernard Shaw's
The Picture of Dorian Grey.

V
Oscar Wilde died in Paris (as one should)
at forty six years of age.

He was an attractive man
with long hair.

He said at US customs
*I have nothing to declare
except my genius.*

VI
Yeats' beloved Maude Gonne
refused all his advances and claimed
her refusal gave his poems
the tension and longing that
made them possible.

VII
Ireland's Bloomsday (June 16th)
is named for James Joyce's Ulysses.
I can't wait for October 10th
to be declared *I Am My Own
Orange County* day in America.

VIII
There is a book called
Each Actor in His Ass
by Michaél Mac Liammóir
which undoubtedly
should be read.

IX
At Swim-Two-Birds
by Flann O'Brien
is about a man writing a novel
about a man writing a novel
which includes several characters
who band together to write a novel.

X
Samuel Beckett wrote
in *Three Poems*
I would likely love to die.
I disagree with that sentiment.

XI
Brendan Behan
(no relation)
The drinker
The writer
The sleeper

XII
The guestbook here has no pen.
They probably assume you'd bring one with you.

XIII
George Jameson, of Jameson Whiskey
owned the house which now houses
The Writers Museum, where I am
now standing. (Though, by the time
you are reading this, I am probably
no longer standing there.)

XIV
I want to rearrange the chairs in
the writers gallery room to get the room
in shape for any event that I might
choose to orchestrate.

XV
A painting of Jonathan Swift
makes him look like Benjamin Franklin
and come to think of it I've never seen
them both in the same place at the same time.

Dublin

Dublin you city of writers
You city of Vikings and rebels
Your failed revolutions
Your faeries your leprechauns

We'd walk the streets with a *Guinness*
in one hand and a *Jameson* in the other
if it were allowed. You're the kind
of people who'd storm a biscuit house
until it was allowed.

You are unseasonably warm,
hiding your rain from the Americans
so it won't embarrass you. We'll talk about
your weather fondly, Dublin.
We'll cross your river. We'll eat
your brown bread.

Dublin, show us your naked Germans
your rock and roll, your Trinity
your old and new, your buildings
built on Vikings.

Show us where you
kiss the sea.

At the Jameson Distillery

I
Jameson Whiskey is triple distilled.
I rarely have the patience to distill anything
more than once.

II
Sine Metu
the Jameson
family motto
means
without fear
which is how we
drink the free
samples.

III
The guide tells us selfie sticks
are banned on the tour and that was
John Jameson's dying wish.
He also says pictures of him (the guide)
are quite valuable.
I question his credibility.

IV
The guide tells us
*If you touch the original mill stone three times
you will have good luck for ten years.*
We'll let you know in ten years
how this worked out.

V
The French lose
a higher percentage of
alcohol to the angels.

VI
I learned a lot about how they make whiskey
on the Jameson Distillery tour.
Then I promptly forgot it all after
the tasting at the end.

VII
Pretty much anything I say after the whiskey tasting
is greeted by Addie's *raised eyebrow of judgment*
which I am now referring to as the *eyebrow of happiness*.

VIII
I'd like to trick some barley
into germinating.

IX
After the tasting you get a whiskey, if you like whiskey
or a cocktail if you don't like whiskey. But I ask you
if you don't like whiskey, why did you come
on the whiskey tour? Please tweet your answers
to @jamesondistillery

X
A man wears a *Jack Daniels* t-shirt
on the Jameson Whiskey tour...
And the second great Irish revolution
begins.

Crack Bird

is not the name
of the restaurant.
It's *Cracked Bird*.
They only serve chicken.
We are not going there.

The Editorial Process

Addie asks what the lamps in *Woollen Mills*
are made of. I tell her jet engines and larger lamps.
She smiles and shakes her head so I guess
that passes the litmus test of whether or not
to include that exchange in this book.

At Woollen Mills

We dine at a restaurant
at the base of the Ha'Penny Bridge
which will cost us much more
than a Ha'Penny. Lucky us.
It's not even the original bridge,
reconstructed not too long ago,
different steel and all, so it wouldn't
break when people crossed it.
Sitting in the middle are people
who would gladly take a Ha'Penny
from you so they could buy a meal
probably not at the restaurant
we are eating at.

Day 5
We Go To Belfast

On the Road to Belfast

I - *haiku*
Our driver Jerry.
He quizzes us on his name.
His name is Jerry.

II
Jerry tells us much of the rebellion
was focused here on O'Connell Street
in view of the giant pole. I assume The Troubles
revolved around those for the giant pole
and those *against* it.

III
Jerry tells us over and over that we're
going to Belfast. He tells people in the street.
He calls his wife and tells her my name is
Jerry and I am going to Belfast. Not really
that last part, but can you imagine.

IV
We drive by the *Irish Yeast Company*.
I have nothing original or clever to say
about that.

V
Jerry's top priority now is to get out of town.
He references John Wayne as one of the first
people to recommend one should get out of town
as quickly as possible. No time to wait for the yeast
to develop its civilization.

VI
Jerry has *no influence on the weather*
he tells another passenger when she asks
what it will be like in Belfast. It will be what it will be
which is a less economical way to say
it is what is.

VII
The signs in Northern Ireland
will not also be in Gaelic, like
they are here in the Republic of Ireland,
which you'll be slapped in the face for
calling *Southern Ireland.*

VIII
The Battle of the Boyne in 1690
is still, to this day, the largest ever fought
on British or Irish soil. May it be this way
forever.

IX
Belfast is a baby city in European terms.
Chartered in the late 1800's, still teething
Still learning what it means to be a grown up.

X
Bunch of cows
lying down
off the side of
the motorway
Pre-tipped or
having a *cow-in*
No time to mingle
with the cows
We're on a green bus
Belfast bound
everything
in this country
is green

XI
Louth is the smallest Irish county
and often referred to as the wee county
so naturally this is where I'd like to establish
my civilization, where, hopefully, they'll see fit
to regard me as their wee overlord.

XII
We enter Northern Ireland.
My seizure of transition does
not go unnoticed by Addie.

XIII
Later on
standing cows
doing the work
the earlier cows
weren't willing
to do

Jerry tells us

if you try to
make a living
selling newspapers
at a church
on a Sunday morning
in Northern Ireland
you'll die of starvation.

Loyalist Bonfire

Wooden pallets
wrapped in green, white and orange
K.A.C. written on the fabric
Kill All Catholics
Effigies of the pope
and Virgin Mary Statue
with face chiseled off
Set on fire
on the twelfth
of July
to provide
maximum insult
Unlike the sensibility
of removed confederate flags
the Protestant Northern Irish say
it's what we do here
and it's not going
to change

Jerry tells us

marching bands in Belfast
can pop up out of nowhere,
shutting down the city.
It's like an infestation or
where marching bands
appear naturally
in the wilds of the city.

On the Black Taxi Tour

I
We take the
Black Taxi Tour
in a yellow taxi.
The rebellion continues.

II
The Peace Wall separates the
Protestants and the Catholics.
It reminds me of the Tom Lehrer song
National Brotherhood Week.
We sign the wall.
There are no plans to take it down.

III
David the Protestant
married a Catholic Girl.
Lost friends as a result.
*At least meet her and
let her offend you
before you judge*
he tells us.

IV
The Protestants say they're
more British than the British.

V
I've got a case of *the troubles.*

Modernism

I
Dyson Air Blades have made it to Belfast City Hall.
I dry each hand in two different ones so
no one can accuse me of taking sides.

II
Autocorrect changes *Dyson* to *dysentery*.
Probably not something they want to
include in their marketing materials.

The Titanic Experience

I
The Titanic Experience begins with a cable car ride.
You take an elevator ride to get to the cable car.
Basically this is the Disneyland of Titanic experiences.

II
My lengthy explanation of how
they have space to build the Titanic
at Versailles does not sit will with Addie.
(She does agree we wouldn't have space
at our house though.)

III
The spinning child
from before the elevator
is back in full force.

IV
One of the cars on
the Titanic ride doesn't work.
Can anyone say *Titanic?*

V
The Titanic's sister ship was *The Olympic.*
She lived a long life and then was
disassembled for parts.

VI
A sign here warns
Robots have come to Titanic.
At least I think it's a warning.

VII
Bandaids here are called
sticky plaster.

Jerry Receives a Call

asking if there are any vegetarians
staying overnight at the bed and breakfast.
He thinks it's a joke as he's never received
such a call. He tells us he'd be eating his
bacon and sausages laughing at us,
but then acknowledges we also
might be laughing at him.
We haven't the heart to tell him
we'd be weeping.

Jerry Points out a Heavily Armored Police Vehicle

He tells us *they all have to be that way because of The Troubles.* We then, almost immediately, see one made out of a Toyota which I feel I could crush with my little finger.

P.S. Haha *Game of Thrones* fans, *Littlefinger...*
 they film that shit here.

That *Wee Cafe* on Falls Street

So much glorious *wee* in the north.

There's a Pizza place in Belfast Called *Big* Caesar's

Oh, it's on.

Danger!

St. Anne's Cathedral has a spire coming out its
middle which looks like *the pole* in Dublin.
(Surely it has been established by now that *The Spire*
on O'Connell Street I refer to as the pole.)
Like the pole was there, and the Cathedral
fell out of the sky, impaling itself on the *Belfast Pole*.

(I want there to be poles everywhere.)

This has been our fear all along,
wherever poles are, that giants might
fall out of the sky and hurt themselves
...on the poles.

Location

There's a sign dead center
in the middle of town
that says "Visit Belfast."
I feel this is not the best place
for this sign.

Made in Belfast

We are eating dessert in shared space
shoulder to shoulder with Catholics,
Protestants, tourists and non-believers.

They happily serve animals who
lived happily near here...That is they are
served on the plates so they could

only be so happy. Something with
chocolate is coming. The clock
on the wall tells me nothing.

A new diet is hard

especially when the restrictions
dictate that your best bet at the restaurant
is to ask them to bring you an empty plate.
Addie is doing the best she can.

I Like the Way This Town Eats

At the restaurant the waitress says
we can get a side of green *vag*.
Bring it on Belfast!

We meet our friend Patrick from L.A.

here in Belfast. He works on *Game of Thrones*
and because it's Saturday he can't take us in
to sit on the Iron Throne. But he is large like
a willing giant which makes us both feel like
wee little *Tyrion Lanisters,* and that is good enough.

It's Over

Domino's in Belfast
doesn't close until 5am.
Western Civilization is ruined.

#4thofjulydoneright

Yes America,
even though I'm in Belfast,
I DID wear my red, white and blue
American flag boxer shorts today.

Good Night Belfast

It is midnight
Fourth of July,
eight days before
their celebration of
the Battle of the Boyne
that launched hundreds
of years of *Troubles*.
Gates still close at night.
Bonfires will be lit to burn
effigies of the other side.
In the *shared space* of
downtown, diners of
every belief sit next
to each other.
Food, the great unifier.
We miss the fireworks
and the tall ships.
We midnight our eyes
right on closed.

Day 6
All Men Must Die

Good Morning Belfast

Thinking about yesterday's driver.
Jerry is the only person I've ever met
who said "Heavens to Murgatroyd" with
any kind of sincerity. He said it twice.
Once while driving up to Belfast, and
a second time when he took a wrong turn
in Belfast and ended up in a part of the town
he was not comfortable being in.
Heavens to Murgatroyd. I hope he
made it back to Dublin okay. I can see
him being carried off by Vikings. One of
the last clans on the Emerald Isle.
His green bus set ablaze as they
carry him across the *Carrick-a-Rede* Bridge.
Heavens to Murgatroyd, the last words you
hear him say as coins fell out of his pocket
into the Irish Sea.

Hostel Notes

I
The youth worker staffing the hostel
which, as I said is a hostel, and not
really a *bed and breakfast*

tells us she spoke to the driver and
he is on his way. We're not sure from
where though. Could be another part of town

or Dublin. We could be standing at the corner
of Lisburn and Fitzwilliam Streets for
a very long time time.

II
The one good thing about
the breakfast they brought us
is that we are staying right
across the street from
Belfast City Hospital.

III
This break-fast
it makes me
more want to
assemble a fast
rather than
break one.

On the Bus

I
When the driver asks
who the best soccer player
in the world was, he was
not surprised when someone
answered *Pele*, though his
whole point seemed to be
that Pele was not from
Northern Ireland.

II
Here's to a time when
all space is shared space and all
the walls are torn down.

III
Let's remove the word
international from the
vocabulary.

IV
They allow cyclists
[on the road] which,
our driver says
is quite crazy.

V
I assess the situation
in case we have to spend
the rest of our lives in
these two bus seats:

We control the curtains!

VI
We're driving to the *Dark Hedges*,
over two hundred years old, twisted *snakey* trees.
Serves as the *King's Road* in *Game of Thrones*
and, I understand, where they will behead
one person from each tour group
for the sake of the fans.

VII
I left my water bottle in Belfast.
Another casualty of *The Troubles*.

VIII
I haven't forgotten
about you Blarney Stone.
I'm just playing coy.

IX
I wonder if they have
dark bathrooms by the
Dark Hedges.

Future Airport Conversation

No.
I have nothing to declare.
Except this cute baby cow
I found near a bridge in Northern Ireland.
Will that be a problem?

Pudding

Pudding
means dessert here.
It also means *pudding*,
which is dessert.
All hail the Möbius strip
versatility of pudding.

All Men Must Die

I
I'm at the point where
while traveling about Northern Ireland
I want to behead myself
to demonstrate my
Game of Thrones
fanmenship.

P.S. *Fanmenship* is now a word.

II
I head into the bathroom
at the *Fullerton Arms* in Ballentoy
for my own *Game of Thrones*.

Painting the Irish Sheep

They paint the male sheep
so they can tell which one is
the father based on what color paint
the females have on them.

I suggested we use a
similar technique before we
made our son which almost led
to us not making our son.

The Story of Fin McCool

I enjoy the story of the Giants Causeway
more than than causeway itself.

Fin McCool, the giant who built a bridge to Scotland
to defeat their Giants. Halfway across the bridge

he sees their giant approaching, who seems much
bigger than he imagined. Fin retreats to

his house where his giant wife disguises
him as a baby. When the Scottish giant arrives

he finds a two hundred foot baby and runs back
to Scotland, imagining the size of the father

destroying the the bridge on his way back.
The remaining stones don't do justice to

the idea of a giant's bridge. The science says
they are leftover lava flow. They do continue

to Scotland under the water. It would be fun
to swim that path, or maybe take a submarine.

I'd rather see giants than
their leftover stones.

Go Away

The weather is amazing at The Giant's Causeway. Especially if you think torrential downpours are amazing.

Ireland is so Green

It makes Kermit the frog
feel inadequate

So green all *frog-in-a-blender* jokes
are no longer relevant.

So green salads in the United States
are on year-long waiting lists to
get visas to enter the country.

So green the colors yellow and blue
mixed together display the pride only
parents can know.

So green Leprechauns,
well they do just fine.

Houses of the Holy

We take photos at Dunluce castle
as featured on the cover of Led Zeppelin albums.
I tell our guide that Zeppelin rules.
He smiles like he already knows.

Fleeting Whiskey

We pass so close to
Old Bushmills Distillery, I can
almost taste the Christmas cake
our guide's mother made, inadvertently
using his thirty-eight year old bottle of
Bushmills Extra Rare Reserve.
We don't stop but, I'll always remember
the story of what he imagined
that whiskey to taste like.

haiku trilogy

I
Addie sleeps as we
roll past Irish cows and sheep.
An Irish bog too.

II
It's always almost
raining in Ireland. Except
when it's not raining.

III
They drive on the left
here, which does not seem *right*. Ha
ha ha ha ha ha.

I Like Big Boyne

We see a bull climbing on top of a cow getting ready to celebrate the anniversary of the Battle of the Boyne in his own way.

Even in the Afterlife

The main Belfast cemetery has three plots,
one for the Catholics, one for the Protestants,

and one for people who died from the flu.
Down the center of that plot, further dividing

the Catholic and Protestant flu victims
is a wall which starts at the surface

and goes twenty feet underground.
So, in death, they would not have to mingle.

Here in Belfast, hatred runs at least
twenty feet deep.

I would Call this Poem *Homeward Bound* if I lived in Dublin

We should be back to Dublin by 8:00.
That's 20:00 in Leprechaun hours.

One last stroll through Dublin

I get so nostalgic about places I just met.
Temple Bar, like a Quartier Latin turned up all the way.

Trinity College, somehow we toured you three times.
I want to enroll and then never go to classes.

O'Connell Street, we tried our best to avoid you
but you cut through the city like an elephant in the room.

Molly Malone, fictitious but every woman's story.
Oh, Molly, people climb on you like they paid for you.

Oh Guinness and Jameson, have you two met?
In every pub you commingle like distant cousins.

Oh Liffey, what city could be mentioned without its
lifeblood river. Los Angeles doesn't count. It's hardly a city.

It's a cacophony of neighborhoods without a centre.
We're not in love with you Dublin but

we'd come out for a walk and a pint every week.
We'd be your close friend. We could trade babysitting

if you bring your kids.
I hope we meet again.

The distance is so inconvenient
but let's keep in touch.

You never know.
The Vikings may come to California

and we'll need a place to go.
Oh water of life

Oh fiery red hair.
Salante!

Salante!

Whiskey all gone
Addie say.

Want another?
I say.

No
She say.

She
very good.

At the Oliver St. John Gogarty Pub

The traditional Irish singer,
a young man
who talks in detail about how
he's been to St. Louis

asks if anyone in the room
is from Spain.
One of his drunk friends
in the back raises his hand

and he responds with
*yeah, you're about
as Spanish as my granny.*
He launches

into a song about
a Spanish man who
wandered into Dublin
and loved a woman.

Isn't that the premise
of all songs?
The accent prevents me
from learning if it worked out.

I hope it did.
Next he asks if
anyone is Scottish.
A few cheers from
a group by the window

and he answers
you dirty liars.
He's glad they're there
as he'd rather dedicate

the song to the Glasgow Boys
instead of to *Shrek*.
Next it's a few tunes for
the guys from Germany.

It's more
traditional Irish music.
I hope they
liked it.

I never
want to leave
this room

We drift out
shortly after
the St. Louis
Ladies.

When we get up to leave
the singer asks us not to.
Get back he says.
I don't know

how we talked
our way out of there.
But we're not there now
so we must have.

In Gogarty's Pub

Several men have Finbarr's beard.
Did I tell you I met an Irish Man
named *Finbarr?*

Day 7
Romancing the Blarney Stone

Good Morning Dublin

I
We're confident the sculpture
in the dining room at the Morrison Hotel
would delight our six year old because of
her superbly pronounced naked butt.

II
Good morning Dublin!
We're leaving you today
to take our chances on the left side
of your rainy roads.

Advice from Patrick

Sit in the right.
Then left left left left
left left left.

Making Myself Pretty

Today I'm going to kiss the Blarney Stone
I wonder if she'll kiss me back. (And if it's a she.)

P.S. No tongue.

P.P.S. *Tongue Kissing the Blarney Stone* also would have been a good title for this book.

Back at the Airport

Our taxi driver
takes the "swords" lane
as we arrive at the airport.
The *Game of Thrones* theme
fills my head and I think
good, yes, good.

Two Ways to Say This

I
One could die of death
waiting in line at the rental car place
at the Dublin airport.

II
We turn into skeletons
waiting to get our rental car.
It's kind of cute though:
matching Rick and Addie skeletons.

Driving to Blarney

I
I start to take this
stay to the left thing too seriously
and end up in Scotland

II
Addie tells me
she's going to have to
put her finger *back in this thing*.
I have no idea what she's talking about
but I can't wait to find out.

III
I'm getting used to driving on the left
while sitting on the right, but the seatbelt
is uncomfortably digging into my neck
which may lead to my beheadation.

IV
No issue at all driving on this side.
Outside of an ancient castle toppled,
the *Rock of Cashe*l melted, and
every hair I've ever come in contact with
turned grey.

Romancing the Blarney Stone

I
I have to walk under a ladder
to enter the loo inside Blarney castle.
The ladder operator assures me
I'll be fine.

II
We walk into Badger's Cave.
No badgers to be seen but I tell Addie
always kiss in a cave. She tells me
she'll add it to the list which currently includes
when crossing a river and everywhere in Paris.

III
We're trying to decide whether
to have lunch in the *Poison Garden*
or at the cafe. Trip Advisor tells us
everything in the Poison Garden
is vegetarian.

IV
First sign inside the castle indicates
there's a *murder hole. Well we'll have to see
The Murder Hole* I tell Addie. Her laughter
tells me she agrees.

*The murder hole was a special stone at the entry way
that visitors would stand on. If the guards didn't like you,
they could release a catch which would cause the stone
to move and you would fall below into a hole. If all went
as intended, you'd be murdered.*

V
I tell Addie we should build a *murder hole*
back at the house. She tells me it won't work
because we don't have a second floor
for someone to fall through.
It's important to note that this is her
only problem with the idea.

VI
Poison Garden
Murder Hole
We see a large metal bowl
That I assume is the
Castration Bucket.

(Not to mention the
Alcove of Defenestration,
The Stairway of Plague Infusion
and the *Pigeon of Magoomba*.)

VII
The line is too slow
for us to coordinate
taking a good shot of me
flung into the murder hole.

VIII
Winston Churchill kissed the Blarney Stone
and unless they've been using sanitary wipes
after each kiss by association we all will have
kissed him.

IX
Kissing the stone
hoping for eloquence
a strange man holds me.
I lean back, my hands on
the poles of safety,
my lips touch the stone
right in front of my wife
the cold stone.

X
We discover the *hello hole*
on the way down from the top
of the castle, though I don't
remember what it was, so
it's possible we just
made it up.

XI
At the cafe when she confirms
that I want the "vag" quiche
I say *oh yes, that's the one.*

XII
I'd like to tell you I tongue kissed
The Blarney Stone, but I won't.
Not because it's blasphemous.
It's not. It's mainly because
it didn't have a tongue.

Driving to Limerick

I
After the Irish coffee in Blarney
I laugh with the gift of eloquence
all the way to Limerick.

II
Addie Demands I write a Limerick in Limerick
I'm not sure this is the kind of thing
our Ketubah covers.

III
We drive through Buttevant.
Whatevant?
Buttevant.

IV
We see a yellow sign
on the road to Limerick
with a cow on it that
we're pretty sure the
locals refer to as a
cowtion sign.

The First Thing I Notice in Limerick

My wife is gluten free
and dairy free but not at all
beautiful free.

haiku

So many wild Swans
looking for food underneath
the Shannon River

24

In Limerick,
the audible indicator
that let's you know it
is safe to cross the street
is a rapid beeping that, if
you are conditioned by TV,
as I am, sounds like the
sound a bomb will make
just before it blows up.
The effect here, for me
anyway, is that I cross
the street rapidly.

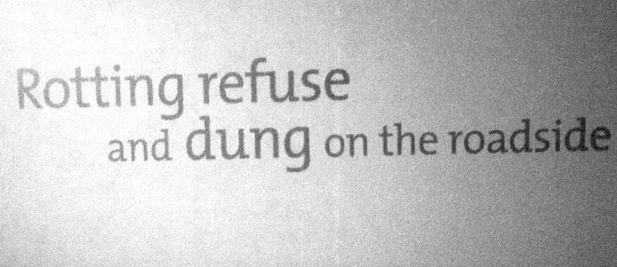

Day 8
A Day in Limerick!

At the Vegetarian Place on O'Connell Street

The sun will be in and out today,
mixed with segments of *proper Irish weather*.
The last thing we want to see is the knees
of an Irishman.

Sausages are coming. Vegetarian ones.
Not made out of any of the animals we've seen
up and down the counties of the Republic.
I'm already the mayor of our hotel. I'm consolidating
my power here in Limerick.

Will be inside a castle soon.
King John is long gone, so I figure it's my time.
A scrambled tofu my crown.
The local swans my inner circle.

Still at the Vegetarian Place on O'Connell Street

Little orange haired Irish babies are everywhere!
Like the toddler who scaled two entire steps
to approach our table at breakfast, the smile
of accomplishment on his face worth the entire
trip overseas. Later he comes back with a little girl
slightly smaller than him, holding hands up the steps.
He's presenting her to us for our approval.
We give our blessing. Send them back down
the stairs for a lifetime of breakfasts
a grape in her right hand.
The Republic lives on.

haiku at the Vegetarian Place on O'Connell Street

It's like a toddler
moshpit up in here. Vegan
restaurant disco.

Parental Intervention at the Vegetarian Place on O'Connell Street

The moms build a barrier of strollers to block the toddlers, which traps us on the upper level of the restaurant. We could just move one of them but we don't want to be presumptuous so we'll just have our mail forwarded here instead.

In the Bathroom at the Vegetarian Place on O'Connell Street

There's no light in the men's bathroom.
But I remember my Jedi training and
it all works out okay.

At the Hunt Museum

I
Note to self:
Addie wants a drinking horn
like the one from the fifteenth century
with the little bird feet.

II
Addie sees the display of small boxes
labeled *caskets* and is concerned humans
wouldn't fit in them, so she designates
a small animal for each one.
The top one is for a mouse.

III
Addie's plan is for the rain to stop
when we're done with the museum.
I think it's a good plan.
Do you hear that sky? She asks.
I have an umbrella ready in case
the answer is no.

IV
Breton Woman
Roderic O'Conor, c. 1896

Looks like *Whistler's Mother*.
But it's not. Maybe it's her
estranged Aunt Murgatroyd.

V
The Artist and His Wife
Robert Fagan, c. 1803

The artist and his wife.
Both dressed for dinner.
Except she has no shirt.

Let's go to dinner.
I'll have the soup.
I bet the waiter
brought her anything
she wanted.

VI
Addie announces she wants
to eat and drink off of pottery
for all of her meals after seeing
the impressive selection from
the thirteenth century in the
Hunt Museum.

Handmade would be ideal,
she adds.

VII
There's a poetry reading here on Wednesday.
The flyers says there will be *finger foods*.
When free food is involved, attendance
among poets will be high.
(Also the attraction of fingers.)

VIII
I win the contest of opening parallel drawers
to see which side had the more interesting
things inside. I think Addie threw the game
as she wasn't willing to take a point for the
green velvet in her bottom drawer, trying
to convince me my spearheads were better.

IX
Addie starts to rush through the museum
as she thinks more and more about the
coconut ball in her backpack.

X
The look of the Bronze Age shield
has me wanting to refer to it as
The Shield of Boobathia.

XI
There's a free *handling session*
in the next room.
We are on our way.

XII
The sign pointing us to the Iron Age display
has a photo of a chicken on it. Perhaps
it's a typo and were actually about to see
the *Chicken Age.*

XIII
Poor Vikings
Their swords and axes
on display in museum cabinets.
They used to be in charge around here.
Now they all live modest lives
in Minnesota.

XIV
The *hands on* exhibit
features combat items.
I'm handed a sword.
Feels good I tell the docent.
Later I found out he's just an intern
I slay him with the sword to
demonstrate proper class structure.

XV
Addie eats a
coconut ball
at the bottom of the
Red Stairway.

XVI
Addie enters the Christ room
immediately after eating the
coconut ball. She asks me to
check her face for chocolate
as Jesus would have wanted.

XVII
Addie can't decide
in the *immaculate conception* room

which piece she likes better,
The little grown man

sitting on a big woman,
or the Madonna holding a child

who has no head or torso.
It's a tough call.

XVIII
The Hunts proudly displayed their collection
of artwork and artifacts in their home, often
blending items from different time periods for
a unique aesthetic. They donated their collection
to the people of Ireland, and for the benefit of
my wife and I as we walk through their past
and settle with a pitcher of water
in their customs house cafe.

Another Rejected Title for This Book:

Feck!

At King John's Castle

I
And now an exhibit in King John's Castle called
Rotting Refuse and Dung on the Roadside
Wonderful, wonderful!

II
Surely they planned this:
The display of heads on stakes
right above a sign that says
Head this way.

III
We learn what the word undermine means.
I don't want to ruin the surprise for you,
so get excited for the revelation when
you visit King John's Castle.
(Don't tell me if you just look it up.)

IV
The strange words I'm getting as a result
of the marriage of typos and autocorrect
are undoubtedly how Gaelic was invented.

V
Joining a crusade
offered a chance to
see the world and
kill the people in it.

VI
Addie is disappointed
there are no cannonballs in
the interactive *Destroy the Castle* exhibit.

VII
Proper Irish weather in July
equals winter in LA
I'm freezing my Judaism off
here in King John's castle.

VIII
Later on we learn
the origins of the word *blacksmith*
and that the word *whitesmith* exists.

IX
The costumed *siege girls* tell us about
the bodies buried beneath the castle.
Unearthed in the pursuit of archaeology.
Covered back up in a proper fashion.
The people who put the mummies in museums
could learn from this.

X
A Canadian takes a picture of us with the siege girls.
She says *everyone say "shit and syphilis"*
which, she says, *usually makes everybody smile*.
One of the siege girls asks *do you get a lot
of photos with confused faces? We usually
tell people to say "siege"*.

XI
Addie pulls a *Rick* when I turn a corner
and discover her head sticking out of a hole
(Though technically I think my uncle invented
that in late nineteen-seventies Syracuse with
the monster mask around his head sticking up
out of the kitchen floor while he was standing
in the basement. (It's possible the monster
was named *Harold*.)

Sipping Tea at King John's Castle

I'm thinking of mines and tunnels
of turrets and stones. The men who
made coin here, who left their pistols
underground not to be discovered for
three hundred and forty eight years.
I'm thinking of the siege and the souls
who never left the castle, buried under
its gravel. The long gone British barracks.
Everything changes, even new things from
the twentieth century. Let's dig a mine.
Let's flood the mine. The Gaelic natives.
Their culture vanishing. I'm sipping tea in
King John's Castle. Irish Breakfast
of course.

King John Never Visited the Castle Named For Him

He should have stopped by.

haiku

It's all fun and games
until a wind blows you off
the Cliffs of Moher.

At the Cliffs of Moher

So pleased they are not named
The Cliffs of Mohel.

I assume it is a beautiful day here
underneath these clouds and fog.

The majesty of these precipices
shuts me right up, which, if you've

been reading, you know is necessary.
The weather is fogging with us

but eventually lifts and we can see them,
cliffs for giants, last step before a long swim

to Philadelphia. Ireland doesn't want us
to see home, shows us these magnificent

beauties to convince us to stay. Even the
cheese plate in the cafe works like

a magnet on me. This cheese probably
made from cows within ten miles of these cliffs

maybe from the milk of the cows we passed.
This is one of the places on the long list

of eighth wonders of the world.
Well, Cliffs of Moher, you've got our vote.

Tell me where to sign my name.
Sorry I have to return to America tomorrow

But you've turned my eyes Irish.
I hope they see you again.

She's Catching On

Addie immediately doesn't believe me when I tell her you can buy a full size replica of the cliffs in the gift shop.

I say Goodbye to the Cows of Moher

Earlier Addie told me, after she caught me
mooing at the cows next to the cliffs, that
I wasn't going to be able to convince them
to come to me. I've been away from cats for
so long. I just need something to pet.
On the trail back down, being careful
not to let the wind blow me into the Atlantic,
a calf, maybe a teenage cow, is waiting by the fence
like she heard me calling, a faint familiarity
with whatever I was mooing.

If Rabbi Nachman of Bratzlav were Irish he would have said

the whole world is a very narrow Irish road.
The most important part is to not have fear.
Tall grass enters the car as we pretend to
be in two-way traffic.

The Limerick Institute of Technology Acronym Spells LIT

Make your college plans now Irish stoners!

Cute Hoor

In the Locke Pub in Limerick
they serve a beer called *Cute Hoor.*
It's my last night so I'm obligated to get a Guinness
but I would like to have the experience of asking
for a *Cute Hoor* out loud to see if the bartender
notices the wildness in my American eyes.

In The Locke

We've been staring at a painting of
Arthur Guinness which turns out to
be a video screen. Every fifteen minutes
he moves. One time he shows you how
to pour a Guinness, another time he
sneezes, and another he pulls out a
copy of *Deceased Brewer Magazine*
and reads it like it's a Playboy, his
tongue out of his mouth, licking his lips
when he gets to the centerfold. We
don't stick around to see everything
he does. There's only so much time
and America beckons.

Ready?

R: Are you ready?
A: To go to the airport?
R: No. To go back to the room.
A: Are YOU ready?
R: I don't ever want to leave this room.
A: Then you're not ready.

Day 9
America bound

Time Travel

Addie asks if we're going back in time
Not in the Marty McFly sense I tell her.
Somehow this flight across the ocean
Will only take two hours, but still that's
forward when all is said and done. Will
all ever really be *said and done?*

One Last Irish Road Sign

A sign on the road to Shannon Airport says *Expert Traffic Delays*. They must think they are so good at them.

One Last Irish Luggage Sign

The pilot tells us it will be eighty-seven degrees.
I can't wait to experience summer weather on
this summer vacation. I'm going to get off this
plane and take off all the clothes America
will legally allow me to remove. No offense
proper Irish weather, and with all due
deference to the perils of global warming;
this boy needs some heat. Bring it on.

I Shed a Tear

Oh proper American toilet seat covers!
I spent the last week building replicas
of my ass out of toilet paper in every
bathroom in Ireland. I salute you America!
Your every miracle.

Lost and Found

Oh crap
I think as we head
to baggage claim.
I left my will to live
on the Cliffs of Moher.

BLARNEY CASTLE, ON THE MIDWAY.

Day I Don't Even Know Any More, Probably Ten

Blue Sky

I'm sitting in the Blue Sky Cafe in Bethlehem, Pennsylvania
with an Ireland hangover and a Lehigh Valley cup of coffee.

Addie tells me she is going to share a bowl with her mom.
She means *Chipotle* and I have no business thinking

anything else. I've got pills laid out in front of me, at
least one vitamin and a red one which is supposed to

make my pain go away. The screaming baby doesn't
help, the clinking of every plate in the restaurant,

the fans above, every one going like a lazy tornado.
Who needs weather indoors? The waiter thinks

I'm an idiot for not seeing the half and half on
The table in front of me. The radio sings about

a girl who dances in the sand half the world away.
That's where I was yesterday, half the world away.

I'm going to sit here, sipping coffee until
my headache goes away. Then I'll leave

this room with paintings hanging on its walls
to go to another building with the word *museum*

in its name.

At the Allentown Liberty Bell Museum

I didn't expect to be immersed in Liberty Bell history at the end of a trip to Ireland, but the photograph, from the Bell's 1893 visit to the Worlds Fair in Chicago, of Blarney Castle in the Irish village exhibit lets me know I'm on the right track.

At The Allentown Art Museum

I
Return of the Prodigal Son
Benjamin West, 1772

Father,
please let me live
inside your beard.

II
Head of a Young Woman
John Singer Sargent, 1878-80

Despite the macabre implications
of the title of this painting, it actually
includes much of her torso, and, it seems
the rest of her, just off canvas.

III
Red Cabbages
Maurice Richard Grosser, 1939

Two red cabbages, like lungs
hold stems like hands, the color
of hearts exposed to the air.
A wood block helping their cause.

IV
Lemons
Hans Moller, 1949

Moller's *Lemons*
reminds me of Picasso's women
which makes me wonder if Moller
was attracted to lemons.

V
Coney Island
Milton Avery, 1933

A fat Charlie Chaplin
rests his belly on the waist
of a bathing suited man
or a topless woman with no breasts
which is what gave her, in 1933,
the authority to be topless.

VI
Landscape with Cows
James McDougal Hart, 1887

Easily could have been named
Cows with Landscape.

VII
Licking Licking Paw
Henry Ossawa Tanner, 1886

Finally the children
with their activity papers
clear away and I can view the lion
licking his paw. The sound of a bell
or a gong nearby doesn't compel me
to not wish, the lion was licking me.

VIII
Golden Afternoon
Cleonike Wilkins, 1940

It *is* a golden afternoon for the young man
with the staff of Moses, surrounded by the four
young women in pastel colored short dresses
wet from the nearby pool.

IX
Outside the Limits
Clarence Hollbrook Carter, 1938

Rosie the Riveter sells fireworks
to the locals, a few years before
she got into riveting.

X
I enter the *Butz Gallery*.
Say it out loud with me people
and revel joyously.

XI
Hot Buttered Corn
John Clem Clarke, 1989

And who doesn't love hot buttered corn?
Wall sized! Could feed a family for a week!
Except for our six year old who claims to
not like corn of any kind, though occasionally
we catch him at dinner, his mouth on a cob.

XII
Still Life with Fruit
Cornelius de Heem, 1655/57

I prefer the American *Still Life with Fruit*
in the other room. It includes watermelon,
so, that's the painting I would lick if I somehow
got trapped in the museum overnight.
(Plus it's near the lion.)

XIII
The Young Fisherman
Follower of Frans Hals, 1635

I first misread the title of this painting as
The Young Frankenstein. I have nothing
to say about this painting after I realized
my mistake.

XIV
Saint Margaret with the Dragon
Heinrich Yselin, about 1478

A sculpture of the original
mother of dragons
with all due respect to
Daenerys Targaryen

XV
Bean eater
Annibale Carraci, 1582/83

With his floppy hat
and red shirt with white collar,
this bean eater was the Gilligan
of his day.

haiku

Car to the airport
I'm all out of poetry
Los Angeles soon

Are You Going to Ireland, My Friend?

for Brendan Constantine

Are you going to Ireland, my friend?
I'd give you a list of things you simply
must do, but I know you'd ignore it
with your special diet and your familial
sensibility. But if you could, just once
stop by Molly Malone? See how her
cleavage is shinier than the rest of her
from all the people (admittedly like me)
who choose to put their hands there
for their photos. If you could just do
that, so the fantasy of us touring the
world together would be a little more
believable. She's in Dublin. You'll
find her in the shadow of a church
where people no longer pray, in the
heart of the city. I hope you meet my
friend Finbarr, if not so we win another
round of the social geography game,
but so you can see his beard. I hope
he still has it. He pretends for a living

and that sometimes requires him to defer to what other people say should be on his face. If you meet him in the ideal circumstance, you'll follow him through the streets where, every now and then, he, and his partner, will stop to tell stories and recite poetry from the Irish masters. Don't let the beard distract you from the words. Don't let the rain get you down, and don't worry, the Irish tax payers will cover your fee every time you cross the Ha'penny Bridge. Ireland my friend. They'll treat you like a God there. They'll paint your blue eyes green. They'll never be able to out-nice you but by God they'll try. It's what they do. It's what you do. You've never seen a country so green.

One Last Thing

Underneath the Snapple cap
at gate C24 in Philadelphia

it says *The original Cinderella
was Egyptian and wore fur slippers.*

Why don't you think about that
until my next book comes out.

About The Author

The author in Dublin

Two-time Pushcart Prize nominee Rick Lupert has been involved in the Los Angeles poetry community since 1990. He was awarded the Beyond Baroque Distinguished Service Award in 2014 for service to the Los Angeles poetry community. He served for two years as a co-director of the non-profit literary organization Valley Contemporary Poets. His poetry has appeared in numerous magazines and literary journals, including *The Los Angeles Times, Rattle, Chiron Review, Red Fez, Zuzu's Petals, Stirring, The Bicycle Review, Caffeine Magazine, Blue Satellite* and others. He edited the anthologies *Ekphrastia Gone Wild - Poems Inspired by Art, A Poet's Haggadah: Passover through the Eyes of Poets*, and *The Night Goes on All Night - Noir Inspired Poetry*, and is the author of eighteen other books: *Donut Famine, Professor Clown on Parade, Making Love to the 50 Ft. Woman, The Gettysburg Undress* (Rothco Press), *Nothing in New England is New, Death of a Mauve Bat, Sinzibuckwud!, We Put Things In Our Mouths, Paris: It's The Cheese, I Am My Own Orange County, Mowing Fargo, I'm a Jew. Are You?, Feeding Holy Cats, Stolen Mummies, I'd Like to Bake Your Goods, A Man With No Teeth Serves Us Breakfast* (Ain't Got No Press), *Lizard King of the Laundromat, Brendan Constantine is My Kind of Town* (Inevitable Press) and *Up Liberty's Skirt* (Cassowary Press), and the spoken word album "Rick Lupert Live and Dead" (Ain't Got No Press). He hosted the long running Cobalt Café reading series in Canoga Park for almost twenty-one years and has read his poetry all over the world.

Rick created and maintains Poetry Super Highway, an online resource and publication for poets (PoetrySuperHighway.com), Haikuniverse, a daily online small poem publication (Haikuniverse.com), and writes and occasionally draws the daily web comic Cat and Banana with Brendan Constantine. (facebook.com/catandbanana) He also writes the weekly Jewish poetry blog "From the Lupertverse" for JewishJournal.com

Currently Rick works as a music teacher at synagogues in Southern California and as a graphic and web designer for anyone who would like to help pay his mortgage.

Rick's Other Books and Recordings

Donut Famine
Rothco Press ~ December, 2016

Professor Clown on Parade
Rothco Press ~ December, 2016

Rick Lupert Live and Dead (Album)
Ain't Got No Press ~ March, 2016

Making Love to the 50 Ft. Woman
Rothco Press ~ May, 2015

The Gettysburg Undress
Rothco Press ~ May, 2014

Ekphrastia Gone Wild (edited by)
Ain't Got No Press ~ July, 2013

Nothing in New England is New
Ain't Got No Press ~ March, 2013

Death of a Mauve Bat
Ain't Got No Press ~ January, 2012

**The Night Goes On All Night
Noir Inspired Poetry** (edited by)
Ain't Got No Press ~ November, 2011

Sinzibuckwud!
Ain't Got No Press ~ January, 2011

We Put Things In Our Mouths
Ain't Got No Press ~ January, 2010

A Poet's Haggadah (edited by)
Ain't Got No Press ~ April, 2008

**A Man With No Teeth
Serves Us Breakfast**
Ain't Got No Press ~ May, 2007

I'd Like to Bake Your Goods
Ain't Got No Press ~ January, 2006

Stolen Mummies
Ain't Got No Press ~ February, 2003

Brendan Constantine is My Kind of Town
Inevitable Press ~ September, 2001

Up Liberty's Skirt
Cassowary Press ~ March, 2001

Feeding Holy Cats
Cassowary Press ~ May, 2000

I'm a Jew, Are You?
Cassowary Press ~ May, 2000

Mowing Fargo
Sacred Beverage Press ~ December, 1998

Lizard King of the Laundromat
The Inevitable Press ~ February, 1998

I Am My Own Orange County
Ain't Got No Press ~ May, 1997

Paris: It's The Cheese
Ain't Got No Press ~ May, 1996

For more information:
http://PoetrySuperHighway.com/

www.ingramcontent.com/pod-product-compliance
Lightning Source LLC
Chambersburg PA
CBHW071728080526
44588CB00013B/1940